CHANGING BRITAIN
WHERE YOU LIVE
MICHAEL RAWCLIFFE

B.T. Batsford Ltd · London

First published 1994

© Michael Rawcliffe 1994

Typeset by Goodfellow & Egan
Phototypesetting Ltd, Cambridge

and printed in Singapore

Published by
B.T. Batsford Ltd
4 Fitzhardinge Street
London W1H 0AH

A catalogue record for this book is
available from the British Library

ISBN 0 7134 6714 2

British Coinage before Decimalization

Until 1970, when decimal currency was adopted, the pound
was divided into shillings. There were twenty shillings to the
pound and twelve pence to the shilling.

old money	abbreviation	value in new pence*
one penny	1d	less than ½p
sixpence	6d	2½p
half a crown	2s 6d or 2/6d	12½p
ten shillings	10s or 10/-	50p

* Remember that prices are now higher than in the past
because of inflation.

Most readers of this book will live either in a built-up area or within fifteen miles of a town or city. This has not always been so. Two hundred years ago only one in four of the population was a town dweller and it was only with the Industrial Revolution that Britain became urban. By 1851 town and country dwellers were roughly equal in number but by 1901 80% of the population was living in towns.

This book is about our changing environment. We live in Britain at a time when change is very obvious. Firms come and go in the high street, and sometimes this is related to recession, when shops are forced to close. At other times fashion is the reason, with the skateboard shop no longer economic. Due to advances in technology, the retailer formerly selling typewriters now also sells word processors and computers. On the other hand, certain features, such as the patterns of the roads, alter less frequently. When the roads were laid out, they may well have followed existing field patterns, or rights of way across fields. In an area that has not been completely redeveloped, the ever-changing shop front may disguise a much older house.

You may live in a town that has had its central area entirely redeveloped, probably in the 1970s or 1980s. The development may consist of shopping arcades and multi-storey car parks, whilst the old town centre may have been bypassed by a ring road and pedestrianized. Office blocks and high-rise council flats may also

have been built. This is the result not only of fashion (e.g. to redevelop or build high), but also a response to housing needs and the problems associated with the motor car. The local authority may wish to attract large multiple stores in order to keep up their income and maintain prosperity, but such changes may adversely affect small, privately-owned shops which cannot afford the new rents. The conservationist may also want to preserve the old central core of the town and retain buildings of historical interest.

The 1980s saw an increasing concern for the environment and our heritage. Pressure groups were set up to ensure that development was in keeping with the character of the area. Many battles were fought and some were won, others lost. In the typical 1980s development there may well be a traffic-free high street or central area, and some buildings may have retained the original façade whilst the interior has been rebuilt. Thus, in the main street of Stratford-upon-Avon, the façade of an old building has been preserved by Marks and Spencer, who have constructed a modern store behind an eighteenth-century front wall.

Development in transport and communication has done much to shape our landscape. Coaching inns have given way to service stations and motels, whilst the petrol or diesel engine has given many people the freedom to travel when and where they like and to live at a distance

from their place of work. This in turn has led to the development of our suburbs and, in the case of London, the Home Counties have become one vast commuter area. Cars are increasingly used for taking children to school, for shopping, leisure and work. Great pressure on the roads has resulted, and much land has been taken in developing new roads, bypasses and motorways. The environmental effects of the motor car in terms of congestion, noise and air pollution are familiar to us all. Train travel is often considered a 'greener' option, but in the 1960s the railways faced severe cutbacks and many of the less profitable lines were closed. The efficiency of the rail service and its cost are a source of constant debate.

In the 1980s choice and market forces became the catchwords of the Conservative administration under Margaret Thatcher who remained Prime Minister throughout the decade. Privatization of state industries, the sale of council houses and the creation of enterprise zones were all introduced. In this way political ideas have contributed to the debate on how change should be effected. The need to rebuild our bombed cities after the war, the need to clear the slums and to house the ever-growing population, and the changing nature of Britain, for example the decline in heavy industry, have all led to discussion as to what should be done. This book is about the changes that have taken place in our built environment.

3

The Industrial Revolution, beginning in the late eighteenth century, has almost invariably been regarded as the cause of our poor urban housing, and everyone has their own image of the Victorian slum. These certainly existed, but equally they had probably always done so. Sections of Tudor London, and London before the Great Fire of 1666, contained areas as bad as anything that followed.

Nevertheless, there were now two very important new differences: the sheer size of the problem and the pace of change. By the middle of the nineteenth century the Industrial Revolution was at its height and coal was the major fuel source for the machinery in large factories and workshops. Job opportunities and better pay drew people to areas such as the North West and the West Riding of Yorkshire, where cotton and woollen textiles were produced. With cheap fuel and a ready supply of raw materials, unskilled workers were employed in the factories, in which the machinery operated twenty-four hours a day. The factory chimneys, and the resultant smoke, were seen as a sign not only of pollution, but of prosperity. 'Where there's muck there's brass' was a northern saying, and while the chimneys were belching out smoke the factories were open and the workers employed.

The great ports and the iron, steel and coal-mining towns were also expanding. By mid-century, with the railways well established, towns such as Ashford, Crewe, Darlington, Rugby and Swindon had emerged as centres for the various railway companies, where the locomotives were built and repaired. The major attractions of such towns were primarily employment and the hope of increased pay. Many migrants also felt that life would be more exciting than in the country. London, as today, was the great magnet, but only led a trend which was mirrored throughout Britain.

The new migrant tried to find housing as near to his or her employment as possible. This was particularly important before the advent of cheap transport and a shorter working day. As a result, accommodation in the already densely packed areas close by the factory, workshop or dock was much sought-after. The level of rent was also important and, along with food, took up most of the wages of the poor. Thus the worker came to live in either low-quality housing, which was quickly run up at the cheapest cost by the speculative builder, or in run-down larger houses, which had been abandoned by those who could afford to move out. In both cases rooms, rather than houses, were rented, however small. Larger houses were sub-divided, with attics and cellars used in addition to the main rooms, which were often divided by cheap partitions or curtains. In this way many families came to live in houses previously occupied by one family and their servants. Even those in 'one up and one down' terraced houses often eased the problem of rent by taking in lodgers.

Not everyone suffered, and there was a minority who gained. Property-owners were able to rent out their land for building development and still receive ground rent. Builders, both large and small, built houses as cheaply and as densely packed together as possible, usually selling to a landlord, who would then charge rent. Thus, 'back-to-back' housing became popular and many areas developed a maze of courts and alleys, ill lit, damp and badly ventilated.

In the past it had been possible to cope as towns, apart from London, had expanded slowly. But by the nineteenth century, parishes, which were not only religious units but the means of local government, found themselves facing unforeseen problems. Many towns as they expanded into the neighbouring villages came to consist of several parishes, each seeking to cope without any central, let alone town, authority. The consequence of such unplanned development was that in the poorest urban areas disease spread rapidly and life expectancy was low. Densely packed, inadequate housing, bad ventilation, dampness, air pollution from the smoke, lack of decent drinking water, inadequate drainage and sewage disposal all became even worse as the population escalated. The inhabitants of the worst slum areas were thought to be dirty and criminal by nature, and a world removed from the respectable classes who lived apart in different districts and who had little real contact with them.

While there were always those who cared for the less fortunate, it was cholera which provided the real spur to reform, largely through fear. The cause of the disease was not known until some fifty years after it entered the port of Stockton in 1831. Within the next year it spread rapidly throughout the country, striking densely populated towns the worst. 'King Cholera' actually spread through water polluted by sewage, affecting the poor most of all, but striking all classes of society. Previously many of those who were comfortably off had had no desire to contribute to

'Where there's muck there's brass'

expensive schemes to solve the problems of poor people, which they thought were of their own making. The spread of disease helped to modify such views.

In 1832 the middle classes gained the vote and three years later the Whig government introduced the Municipal Corporations Act, which enabled towns and cities with charters to have their own councils, elected by the householders. The councils were able to levy a rate and introduce bye-laws. In addition, the new Poor Law Act of 1834 took the administration of poor relief away from the parishes and placed it in the hands of elected Boards of Guardians.

Following the cholera outbreak, Parliament commissioned several reports. The first and most important was largely the work of one man, Edwin Chadwick, who, drawing on information supplied by the Poor Law medical officers, produced a report entitled *An Inquiry into the Sanitary Conditions of the Labouring Population of Great Britain in 1842*.

It was yet another outbreak of cholera in 1846–7 that led to the first real piece of legislation, the 1848 Public Health Act. This enabled local Boards of Health to be set up in areas with a high death rate, at the request of a majority of rate-payers. Once the Board was established, rates could be levied for health improvements such as drainage schemes. Bye-laws could also be introduced to regulate new buildings and roads.

Much Victorian legislation was permissive, allowing local councils to act, rather than requiring them to do so. For example, the Artisans' Dwellings Act of 1875 allowed councils to demolish slums where necessary. In time councils came to regulate not only public health, but also town planning. In Sheffield the building of new back-to-back houses was banned in 1862. In other areas rates were raised for redevelopment. In this Birmingham took the lead under Joseph Chamberlain, and in the 1860s forty acres of the town centre were cleared and redeveloped.

By the end of the century there was still much to be done, but local government had come to recognize and take responsibility for the problems.

Industrial Sheffield in 1885. Note the two steel furnaces behind the workers' cottages and the canal in the foreground. How many examples of pollution can you identify?

Decades of Rapid Growth: 1861–1911

The following table, dating from the 1920s, lists towns with a population of over 50,000 that increased in size by at least 25% between census years (i.e. over a ten-year period).

1861–71 Acton, Barrow-in-Furness, Battersea, Birkenhead, Bootle, Bradford, Chesterfield, Croydon, Darlington, Dewsbury, Ealing, Gateshead, Grimsby, Hackney, Hammersmith, Hampstead, Islington, Kensington, Lambeth, Leeds, Leicester, Lewisham, Middlesbrough, Northampton (same rate as 1871–81), Paddington, Poplar, Reading, Rotherham, Sheffield, Southport, Stockton-on-Tees, Swindon, West Hartlepool, Willesden, Wimbledon.

1871–81 Barnsley, Bournemouth, Burnley, Burton-upon-Trent, Camberwell, Deptford, Derby, Eastbourne, Hastings, Hull, Leyton, Lincoln, Luton, Nottingham, Oldham, St. Helens, Salford, Stoke Newington, Tottenham, Warrington, West Ham, Wigan.

1881–91 Doncaster, East Ham, Enfield, Fulham, Hornsey, Newcastle upon Tyne, Newport (Monmouthshire), South Shields, Walthamstow, Wood Green, Woolwich.

1891–1901 Blackpool, Edmonton, Gillingham (Kent), Ilford, Southwick, Southampton, Wallasey.

1901–11 Coventry, Hendon, Southend-on-Sea.

Try and find out why the population of these towns increased so rapidly, and where they are located. Do any regional patterns emerge? Are some towns associated with certain industries?

From Census of England and Wales 1921: General Tables *(1925)*

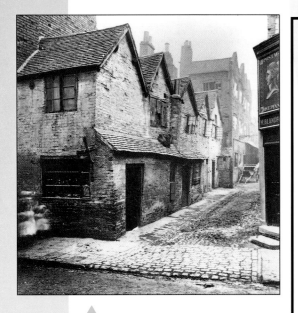

Central Birmingham before redevelopment in the 1860s. The buildings are probably small workshops, for which Birmingham was famous. What clues suggest this? After which date was the inn sign erected?

Profits from the Slums

The courts and culs-de-sac exist everywhere. The building of houses back to back occasions this in a great measure. In one cul-de-sac, there are 34 houses and in ordinary times there dwell in these houses 340 persons . . . but as these houses are many of them receiving houses for itinerant labourers, during the period of hay-time and harvest and the fairs, at least twice that number are then here congregated. . . . in the days of the cholera, 75 cart-loads of manure [were removed] and . . . there now exists a surface of human excrement of very considerable extent, to which these impure and unventilated dwellings are additionally exposed. This property is said to pay the best annual interest of any cottage property in the borough.

Why did itinerant labourers come to stay in Leeds at certain times? What diseases might spread in the conditions described by Mr Baker?

From Mr Baker's account of the conditions of the working poor in Leeds, published in Edwin Chadwick's Inquiry into the Sanitary Conditions of the Labouring Population of Great Britain *(1842)*

Average Age of Death, 1840s

	Liverpool	Manchester	County of Rutland	County of Wiltshire
Professional persons and gentry, and their families	35	38	52	50
Tradesmen and their families	22	20	41	48
Mechanics, labourers and their families	15	17	38	33

What conclusion can be drawn from these figures? What are the possible explanations for the variations between groups and between town and country?

From An Inquiry into the Sanitary Conditions of the Labouring Population of Great Britain in 1842 *by Edwin Chadwick*

Part of the 1847 Ordnance Survey map for the Horrocks district of Preston in Lancashire, an area with many cellar dwellings in which hand-loom weavers worked. Note the density of

◆ through-houses
◀▶ back-to-backs

the housing. How many back-to-back houses can you identify?

1 Nineteenth-century reports on our towns and cities are available from urban archives. Compare one report with a large-scale Ordnance Survey map. (Your local reference library may have Victorian maps.)

2 Look at a Victorian census giving details of the residents of a particular street. (Census returns from 1851 onwards are best.) What are their occupations?

3 A number of museums have displays re-creating urban life in the nineteenth century. You might like to visit one of these, for example the Kelham Island Museum, Sheffield, or the Manchester Museum of Technology (where you can go down into a Victorian sewer).

Whilst agriculture was still the nation's largest employer in 1851, the census of that year also revealed that numbers in town and country were roughly equal. Within thirty years this was to change radically. By 1901, only one in eleven of the employed population was still working on the land; a fifth of this workforce was over fifty-five years of age.

The biggest physical changes to the landscape were in the rapidly growing industrial areas of the North and Midlands, where the towns pushed out into the existing countryside, linking once separate villages. Some parts of the countryside were exploited for valuable raw materials: clay for bricks, coal for fuel and stone and gravel for buildings and roads.

Some areas, particularly between the growing industrial towns, were neither town nor country. Touring England in 1861, the Frenchman Taine described a rural–industrial landscape with polluted streams and dust-covered hedges.

In many ways the demands of the towns helped to change the countryside, and the development of the railway system made this possible. Though the poor may not have been aware of it, the standard of living was rising throughout the century. With this rise, demand increased not only for basic foodstuffs such as vegetables (especially potatoes) but also for meat. Hence wheat, which had prevailed earlier in the century,

Saturday Evening: The Husbandman's Return by W.R. Bigg (1840). Why do you think the artist portrayed the family in this way? Is the painting still useful to a historian?

was often replaced by pasture for cattle. Agriculture experienced a golden age in the mid-century, but in the last quarter found itself subject to competition from the USA and Canada in terms of wheat, and from the Americas and New Zealand in terms of beef. Food imports were now possible over a greater distance due to the development, from the 1880s, of the coal-powered ship and of refrigeration. This competition gave rise to a changing emphasis in agriculture, while from the 1860s the railway led to an expanding home market, enabling distant counties to supply London with milk and soft fruits. Animals and poultry that had been driven along drove roads from the surrounding counties to the London markets were now transported by railway wagons. Many areas with good links to the towns and cities saw a switch from arable to orchards, to hop fields for beer, and to soft fruits.

In 1830 the Swing Riots broke out in the Home Counties, in part caused by the introduction of the threshing machine, and the reduction in the need for labour. The riots took the form of rick and barn burning, which continued into the 1840s. As the century went on, further mechanization took place, with the coming of steam ploughs and combine harvesters. Steam was increasingly used to power the rollers for the production of grain, and deserted windmills became a feature of the Victorian countryside.

Rural crafts also began to decline, since items such as beer barrels could be manufactured more economically in workshops in the towns. Similarly, local breweries found themselves unable, in some cases, to compete with their large urban neighbours.

Local markets were still held, but declined in importance, with competition from the town shops which could be reached by train. The local horse-drawn carrier's van had been the main form of communication for the ordinary person, taking goods from village to village, and carrying passengers at a penny a mile. Now the carrier began to leave catalogues from the town shops and deliver purchases on his return journey. Sometimes he delivered goods from the local railway station.

Before the railway existed, ordinary houses would be built from local materials and regional styles prevailed. Slate roofs were only to be found in areas near slate quarries, such as Wales or the Lake District. In other areas, roofs would be thatched, whilst walls would be made of brick, flint stone or wood, depending on what was available locally. Heavy materials such as slate could now be transported cheaply by rail, and thus many working-class streets in northern towns, far from the quarries, came to have slate roofs.

polluted streams and dust-covered hedges

With cheap excursion fares and shorter working hours, people took the opportunity to spend time in the countryside, perhaps revisiting a life which they or their parents had left not many years before. The fields, surrounded by hedges, were certainly a welcome change for many who worked in the industrial towns. There was a vast exodus from the East End of London every year to work in the hop fields of Kent. In this way, families could have a working holiday and earn extra cash to help them in the hard winter months.

Clearly there were areas far from the railway that remained relatively untouched, in which little agricultural machinery was used, and in which the thatched cottages were far removed from the new buildings of the town. However, for the majority, the landscape and the rural economy were changing. Many cottages, which today would be much sought-after, were in a state of disrepair, or had been abandoned as families moved on. Barns that were once flourishing were left to decay, and in several counties there were clear signs of rural depopulation.

In many ways the hierarchy of the village had been one of its strengths. At the top, the lord of the manor rented land to tenant farmers who would, in turn, employ agricultural labourers. The hours were long, and employment for many was dependent on the weather. The labourer would be expected to attend church regularly with his family and non-attendance might lead to his being evicted from his tied cottage. Agricultural wages were low, especially away from the towns. Accommodation was often made available, certainly in closed villages where the landowner provided sufficient houses only for his own workers. In these estate villages, the population remained fairly constant and the poor rates were thus kept down. In open villages, where there was no dominant landowner, the population expanded more quickly and housing was often inferior. It was from these that much rural migration took place due to insufficient work.

One can see two types of migration through a study of the census: first, the pull of a great town or city such as London, attracting people from large distances. Those who prospered came in turn to move out again to the less crowded suburbs. Secondly, there was short-term migration, where families would move several times over small distances, to settle eventually in the town.

Thus the Victorian countryside was not prosperous, yet neither was it isolated. Over the century, even in the rural areas, the landscape was changing. The only certainty was that many who lived in the growing towns were recent migrants from the surrounding countryside.

Village Dwellings

Hyppolite Taine was a Frenchman who toured England in the 1860s. In these extracts he describes various homes in a village of some 400 people.

Day Labourers' Cottages

Several of the cottages are very poor, being of clay covered with laths, a thatched roof, the rooms are too low and too narrow, the windows too small and the partitions too thin. Think of a large family huddled in winter in one of these rooms, with washing drying . . . The occupant of one of these thatched cottages is a day-labourer, married, the father of six children who earns twelve shillings a week . . . a cottage like this costs from three to four pounds yearly.

The Houses of Carpenters and Carters

Their houses are of brick and covered with red tiles; one of them is flanked with a pretty large garden filled with vegetables, well cultivated, garnished with fine strawberries, with some beehives in a corner . . . The rooms are rather low, but are not wanting in air; the small panes of glass connected by slight triangles of lead allow plenty of light to enter; one goes along a passage of bricks carefully washed to enter the outhouse . . . on the first floor are two bedrooms.

A Farmer's House

His house is old, with a porch in front forming a vestibule; in the hall is antique furniture. The staircase of massive wood, an immense fireplace capable of containing an entire trunk . . . The farmer has twelve huge and superb horses, and a steam threshing machine; among his profits, he sells eighty fat pigs yearly.

From Notes on England *by Hyppolite Taine (1871)*

Why is it unwise to generalize about what rural housing was like? Given the opportunity, which of the above villagers would wish to move or migrate?

An engraving from the Illustrated London News *of 1846. How can you tell that the artist is in sympathy with the family? What makes this cottage poor?*

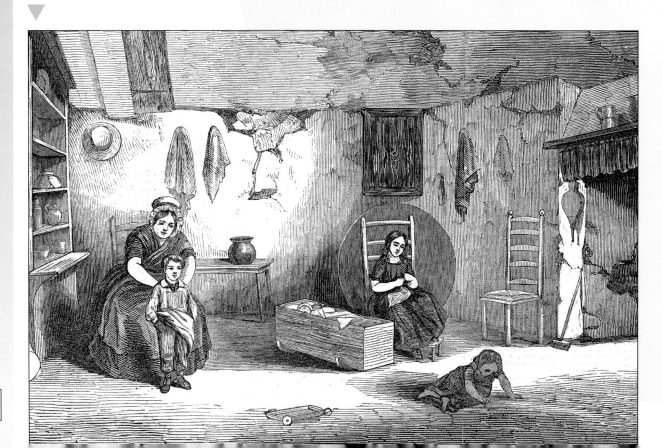

THE HOME OF THE RICK-BURNER.

A Punch *cartoon of 1844. In Suffolk and Norfolk alone there were 302 arson attacks in 1843–4. How does the cartoonist suggest that the devil might be able to persuade the labourer to carry out such an attack? Can you identify the cartoonist's name?*

1 Your local-history library will have various Victorian trade and commercial directories, e.g. Pigot's, White's and Kelly's, giving details of people's occupations.

2 Study the road and inn names in your area, which can often provide a valuable guide to the past (for example, Drovers Road, Milk Street, The Wheatsheaf, etc.).

3 Vivid accounts of country life in Victorian England are given in books such as *Kilvert's Diary*, in which the author describes his life as the curate of Clyro in Wales in the 1870s, and *Lark Rise to Candleford* by Flora Thompson, which is set in Oxfordshire in the 1880s and 1890s.

4 Museums of particular interest to students of nineteenth-century rural life include the Welsh Folk Museum, St Fagans, South Glamorgan; the Weald and Downland Museum, Singleton, Sussex (an open-air museum); the Museum of English Rural Life at the University of Reading; and the Museum of Lincolnshire Life, Lincoln.

Peasantry in Dorset, 1846

A correspondent from *The Times* visited the Dorset village of Stourpaine and his report was published on 25 June:

The first feature which attracts the attention of a stranger on entering the village, is the total want of cleanliness which pervades it. A stream, composed of the matter which constantly escapes from pigsties and other receptacles of filth, meanders down each street, being here and there collected into standing pools which lie festering and rotting in the sun so as to create wonder that the place is not the continual abode of pestilence – indeed the worst malignant fevers have raged here at different times . . . It is by no means uncommon for the whole family to sleep in the same room, without a curtain or the slightest attempt at separation between the beds.

The rents of these hovels vary, with few exceptions, from 1/- a week up to £3 and even £4 per annum.

How do you think this report would have been received by the readers of *The Times*? Do you think Stourpaine was an open or closed village?

In the second half of the nineteenth century there was a growing reaction to the way in which the poor were living in densely populated towns and cities. Since urban centres were increasingly segregated, the comfortable middle classes rarely came into contact with people from the slums, let alone visited a slum. Many had moved out to the suburbs and commuted to work by train or horse-drawn omnibus. The poor were embarrassingly visible even in the prosperous shopping areas, but were usually either selling in the street or begging. Few realized that the gowns, suits and shoes displayed in the windows of the large stores or worn by the lady alighting from her carriage were made in crowded workshops which were

bitterly cold in winter and oppressively hot in summer. The irregular wages earned meant that workers could never escape from the overcrowded slums.

In the 1840s the problems caused by inadequate housing had been exposed by Edwin Chadwick. Many people, if they thought about it at all, assumed either that conditions were generally improving or that those who still lived in abysmal surroundings did so through their own fault. Many were quite prepared to give money to the Church to provide clothing or soup kitchens for the poor, but would not involve themselves further.

However, there were various influences at work. As early as 1799 Robert Owen had created a

Beaconsfield Buildings in Islington, north London. These model dwellings were opened in 1879 and were designed for the poor labourer and his family. Some 2,000 lived in these three blocks, of which many still remain in our large cities.

model village community, providing good housing and education for the workers and their children in his textile mill at New Lanark near Glasgow. Fifty years later, Titus Salt founded a similar village at Saltaire near Bradford. Both employers sought to show that it was possible to provide good rented accommodation for their workers and at the same time maintain a profitable business. Later in the century the two most substantial schemes were those launched by Lord Leverhulme at Port Sunlight and by George Cadbury at Bournville. Thus by the end of the nineteenth century it had been shown that it was possible to provide good housing in pleasant surroundings away from the towns. Up to this point, however, the schemes had been generously supported by individual founders for their own employees – they were not commercial ventures.

Also successful on a small scale was the work of Christian Socialists such as Octavia Hill, who believed that they should not merely accept poverty and give charity to the poor. Rather they sought to alter the conditions leading to the development of the slums and the misery associated with them. Octavia Hill became well known for her work among the urban poor. She believed that open spaces and parks should be provided as lungs within a city, that gardens should be laid out and smoke pollution checked. She came to play a leading role in the Charity Organization Society, which did so much to bring pressure to bear upon Parliament to pass the Artisans' Dwellings Act in 1875.

At a practical level, she took over property in Southwark in south London in 1884 from the Church Commissioners and sought, through education, to show the tenants that even poor property could be improved by painting and decorating and general maintenance. Only those who paid their rents regularly were retained.

In 1863 the Improved Dwelling Company had been formed by Sidney Waterlow and between 1864 and 1890 managed to provide many tenement blocks in central and east London. Today they look very bleak and austere, but they consisted of self-contained flats, had plenty of ventilation and decent sanitation. They managed to produce a 5% annual dividend, achieved largely through the use of large-scale building methods. The company even imported prefabricated windows because these were cheaper. A second commercial experiment was the Artisans', Labourers' and General Dwellings Company, which was founded in 1867 and concentrated on building cottage estates outside central London.

A venture of a different kind was established by George Peabody, an American millionaire, who set up the Peabody Trust in 1862 to provide accommodation in tenement blocks for urban workers and their families. Many of these tenements still survive today. Although the rents charged meant that they were occupied by skilled workers and not the poor, they did help to provide some much-needed homes.

In 1888 the London County Council (LCC) was founded and five years later took the opportunity provided by the 1890 Housing Act to clear a crowded slum area in Bethnal Green in east London. In its place they built the Boundary Estate, where more than 5,000 people were housed, over half of them having two rooms and 37% having three. The estate was built not just to solve a present problem, but to last several generations. Thus the rents again were too high for those most in need.

In spite of these, and other, schemes, many of our towns and cities still suffered from overcrowding at the beginning of the twentieth century. Several studies brought home the problems and conditions of the slums to the general public. One of the most important was that begun by Charles Booth in 1886, mainly to check misleading statements such as those of Henry Hyndman, leader of the Social Democratic Federation (the SDF, a Marxist party), who had said that one-quarter of the population of London was living in a state of poverty.

Booth began his research in the East End of London, and found that 35% of the population there lived in poverty. Between 1889 and 1902 he was to publish seventeen volumes of information on the people of London. One of the most startling facts was that even within the most prosperous boroughs there were pockets of real poverty. Booth was to become one of the advocates of the old-age pension.

Inspired by Booth's work, Seebohm Rowntree, a wealthy York chocolate manufacturer, set out to study his own city.

York was – and still is – a pleasant cathedral market town. Thus it came as a surprise when he found results very similar to those of Booth's study of London. Many people were so poor they could do nothing to help themselves. Old age, loss of a wage earner, or injury at work took families below the poverty line and into what Rowntree called 'primary poverty'.

Thus by the turn of the century, social problems were clearly on the political agenda. However, in 1899 the Anglo-Boer War broke out. Whilst ending in a British victory in 1902, it proved extremely expensive. The Conservative government's plans for old-age pensions had to be abandoned, and it was not until the Liberal victory in the 1906 election that the new ideas came to be put into practice.

good rented accommodation for workers

Rowntree's Findings

Rents Paid by Working-class Families

Number of families	Percentage of the working classes as a whole	Average income, including total earnings of children and other supplementary earners, and payment made by lodgers for board and lodging	Average rent, including rates	Percentage of income paid in rent
714	6	Under 18s (average 10s)	2s 11¼d	29
1,196	10	18s and under 20s (average 19s)	3s 6¼d	18
1,580	14	20s and under 25s (average 23s)	3s 11½d	17
2,828	24	26s and under 30s (average 28s)	4s 6d	16
2,427	21	31s and under 40s (average 36s)	5s 1d	14
1,006	9	41s and under 50s (average 45s 6d)	5s 8d	13
479	4	51s and under 60s (average 55s 8d)	6s 8¼d	12
738	7	Over 60s (average 74s)	7s	9
529	5	Not known		
11,497	100			

NB   Overcrowding was defined in the 1891 census as two or more persons per room.

Why do you think the percentage of income paid in rent is highest for the very poor?

From B. Seebohm Rowntree, Poverty: A Study of Town Life *(1901)*

The Boundary Estate was begun by the LCC in 1890 under the terms of the 1890 Housing Act. It replaced high-density slum dwellings with four-storey flats branching out from a central garden.

▼

Poor Housing

Undesirable housing conditions may be classified under some twelve heads: (1) old property in bad condition; (2) comparatively new houses badly built; (3) property neglected by the owner; (4) property abused by the occupier; (5) houses built upon insufficient space; (6) houses erected on damp or rubbish-filled ground; (7) houses occupied by families of a class for which they were not designed and are not suited; (8) insanitary houses; (9) badly arranged block dwellings; (10) badly managed blocks; (11) excessive rents; (12) crowded houses.

Which of these factors were the fault of (a) the builder, (b) the landlord and (c) the tenant? Suggest how some of the problems might be improved or overcome. Which factors could not be remedied and would then require the property or street to be demolished?

From Charles Booth, Life and Labour of the People in London *(1902)*

1 Look at other parts of either Booth's work on London or Rowntree's work on York.

2 Ask the librarian in your local reference library for any available Victorian inquiries into your area.

3 Try to find an area near you that was built in the nineteenth century and has not been redeveloped. How far have the houses been altered externally?

4 Using a good encyclopaedia, find out more about the life of one of the following: George Cadbury, Lord Leverhulme, Robert Owen, Titus Salt.

5 Look at a daily newspaper for a week and identify problems of housing that still exist today. Are their causes similar to those in the nineteenth century? What solutions are now being proposed?

A nineteenth-century print of Titus Salt's factory and model village at Saltaire, West Yorkshire. Note the River Aire, the splendid factory entrance, the church and the workers' homes.

In 1898 a book was published that was to have an enormous influence on the way we build today, and on planning in general. It was Ebenezer Howard's *Tomorrow: A Peaceful Path to Real Reform*. Howard believed that his idea of a garden city would bring together the best of both town and country. His work was a reaction against the ever-growing expansion of the great cities and towns, and the indiscriminate spread into the countryside, which he thought led to enormous social problems. Howard devised what he called a social city, intending it to be free from the conditions exposed by Charles Booth and others. Like Booth, Howard feared that the countryside was in danger of losing its identity and population. What he sought was a 'town–country magnet'.

Howard's ideal garden city was to have a population of about 30,000. It would be separated from any neighbouring city or town and would comprise low-density housing and amenities such as parks and shops. A particular area was to be designated for industries, so that little travelling to work would be involved. In addition, there would be a rail system that would provide a link with other areas. The garden city would be developed by its own corporation, which would buy land at agricultural prices. This would be less expensive than in urban areas.

As the garden city was developed, land values would rise and the corporation use the 'profits' to provide public buildings, parks and leisure facilities. Thus the garden city would provide its own employment as well as being surrounded by countryside, which in time would give employment to rural workers. In this way, urban sprawl would be avoided by the introduction of what we know today as the Green Belt, in which no building may take place.

Howard's book received wide publicity and eight months after its publication the Garden City Association was founded to promote his ideas. Soon afterwards, Letchworth in Hertfordshire was chosen as the site of the first garden city. Letchworth was situated 34 miles from London in a depressed rural area with low land prices. Some 3,822 acres were purchased, of which two-thirds were retained for agricultural use. Two roads already ran through it, as did a railway line. A temporary station was built in 1902, but it was to be another ten years before permanent buildings were established and a bus service to Luton was instituted. Until then there was only a horse-drawn omnibus.

The experiment had both advantages and disadvantages. The Garden City Association had a free hand to draw up their own plans for the new town. Roads and culs-de-sac were all laid out, as were the public buildings. Gas,

An architect's plan for houses in Hampstead Garden Suburb, north London. Who might be likely to buy houses such as these? Which features would attract the potential buyer? Which design do you find the most attractive? Give reasons for your choice.

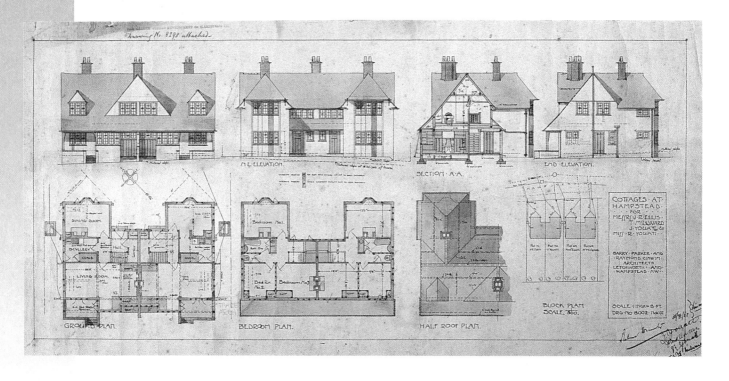

electricity and a sewage works were also provided. As a result a low-density town was created, where each house was set in its own garden and provided with full services. Industries were soon introduced so that people could work within easy reach of home. Thus the Association was able to achieve Howard's dream of combining the best of both town and country.

However, the site was not close to London, and whilst it had a railway goods yard from 1905, it did not have good rail communications. Hence the development of Letchworth was slower than envisaged. By 1939 it had only 17,427 people. Nevertheless, it was a prototype for the future and much was learnt from it. The new towns built after the Second World War owe much to Letchworth.

London itself was continually expanding in every direction, and developers were quick to take advantage of any improvement in communications. Canon Barnett and his wife Henrietta were social reformers who had opposed developers and had managed to resist building plans that threat-ened Hampstead Heath in north London. In 1906, in order to avoid urban sprawl, they acquired 243 acres of land close by the Heath for planned development. This was to be known as Hampstead Garden Suburb. Roads were laid out and houses built, and the scheme was a great success. People who found Letchworth difficult to get to visited Hampstead as an example of a planned garden city. Soon the phrases 'garden city' and 'garden suburb' were indistinguishable, especially as the architect of Letchworth, Raymond Unwin, went to live in Hampstead. The venture was also helped by the extension of the

A modern photograph of housing in Letchworth. Note how the green around which the houses are situated and the mature trees have helped to create a rural atmosphere and a feeling of space.

electric railway to nearby Golders Green. However, Hampstead and Letchworth differed in important respects. Hampstead residents were in fact commuters who used the improved rail link and continued to work in London. In that sense it was really a planned suburb, unlike Letchworth, where industry had been attracted to the town. Thus, only Letchworth fulfilled Howard's original ideal in creating its own employment.

After the First World War, Lloyd George, Prime Minister of the coalition government, called for a large-scale ex-pansion in house building. The new phrase 'homes for heroes', expressing the dream of a better world, spurred on the politicians. Moreover, the Garden City Association tried hard to encourage the government to learn the lessons of Letchworth and to plan development carefully. However, the politicians believed that this would lead to delay and be too costly. Thus the Housing Act of 1919, whilst stating that housing should be well planned and sited, ignored any further advice. In reaction to this, Howard went ahead and purchased land at Welwyn, 21

a prototype for the future

miles from London. A corporation was established to build what later came to be called a satellite town, on garden-city principles. The whole area was planned and certain sectors assigned for industry, housing and agriculture.

Welwyn Garden City was established on 20 April 1926 and was to comprise 40–50,000 people. A branch line had been built in 1920, and in 1926 a main-line station was opened. The development had a mixture of housing. Some houses were built under the 1919 Act, others by private firms, but all under the supervision of the town corporation. The corporation was also successful in attracting industry and, by 1948, film studios, food-processing factories, manufacturing chemists and numerous engineering firms were all located there. In 1948 it was designated a New Town.

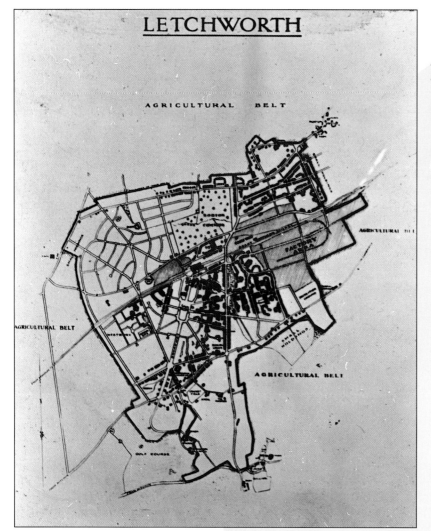

LETCHWORTH

AGRICULTURAL BELT

AGRICULTURAL BELT

AGRICULTURAL BELT

AGRICULTURAL BELT

GOLF COURSE

Letchworth in Hertfordshire, Britain's first garden city, was founded in 1902. How have the planners sought to avoid the problems of the great industrial cities of the nineteenth century? In what ways does this plan (published in 1904) fulfil Ebenezer Howard's ambition to create a 'town–country magnet'? (You may find it helpful to read p. 16 again.)

The Garden City Association

The garden city is not merely an aesthetic [beautiful] idea to provide gardens, nor to force better habit on the people. It is an attempt to secure justice for the people by constitutional means by diverting the increment of value [profit] attached to the land into the pockets of those who create that value. It will help them to educate themselves. It is an experiment of the first magnitude in effective social reform.

It is not a utopian scheme, delightful in theory, but unworkable in practice.

It is a practical scheme . . . and has a sound financial basis resting upon the increase in the value of land caused by the influx of population.

Why do you think that each of the political parties, Conservative, Liberal and Labour, welcomed the scheme? How do garden cities differ from earlier housing schemes described in this book?

From a manifesto of 1902 by the Garden City Association. Quoted in C.P. Purdom, The Building of Satellite Towns *(1925)*

Arguments against Garden Suburbs

Garden suburbs are no solution. They are better than tenements but in the case of London, they have to be so far from the centre that the daily journeys are a grievous burden on the workers. Thousands of people have flocked back to the riverside districts in order to be within walking distance of their work again. Suburban development is costly. Land bought for housing in the London suburbs has cost £700 to £2,000 per acre. The necessary new lines of communication will cost millions. And this method of expansion ignores the needs of industry. Manufacturers carried on . . . in makeshift premises in Central London, cannot hope to be efficient or to meet the legitimate demands of labour.

The greater part of the estate is now farmed, arable crops predominating. The coming of a new large population will create a big demand for produce and much increase the value of the farms and the number of workers in the agricultural belt.

Why must one be cautious about the arguments used in a pamphlet such as this? What other arguments might the writer of the pamphlet put forward? Add a final paragraph of your own.

Preliminary Announcement of a garden city in Hertfordshire for London Industries, *September 1919*

1 If you live near any of the garden cities or suburbs mentioned in this section, look at both the town plans and plans of individual houses (obtainable from the local reference library) and then visit the site.

2 How many of the ideas put forward by the planners of garden cities at the turn of the century are still valid and have been built into today's planning and design?

3 Design an advertisement for a garden city. Make sure you pitch it clearly at either prospective industries and firms or at employees/residents.

4 Explain why each of the following was essential to the success of a garden city: (a) good housing, (b) newly located industries, (c) transport, (d) space, (e) employment and (f) amenities.

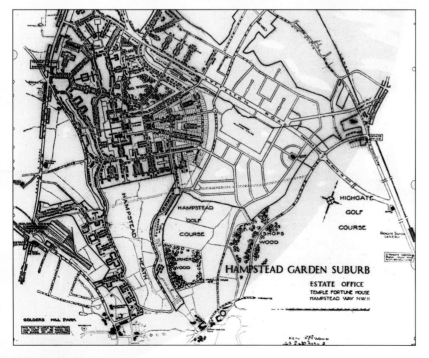

Plan of Hampstead Garden Suburb. Compare this with the plan of Letchworth opposite. In what ways does Letchworth differ from Hampstead? What does this tell you about the difference between garden cities and garden suburbs?

Before the First World War, local authorities had provided only a small proportion of new homes, and between 1900 and 1914 demolition of unsuitable housing had outstripped new building. A town-planning act in 1909 had in theory given local authorities an opportunity to plan schemes for council housing, but by 1914 demand was still high. This led to increased rents. After a rent strike in Glasgow, rent control was introduced. At the end of the war, in November 1918, the government was faced with a dilemma. It wished to free rents from control but could only do this if the supply of houses increased, and if the local authorities played a positive role in house building.

In 1917 the government had established a commission to inquire into housing and in the Walters Report of 1918 it was recommended that development should be on the edge of towns and cities, enabling workers to commute daily to work by cheap transport. This housing was to be low density and, if implemented, the report would have meant the end of overcrowded bye-law terraces. Politicians felt it important that the men who had given so much to the country in war should now have decent housing – in other words, that there should be 'homes for heroes'. What was unsaid was that November 1917 had seen a Bolshevik (Communist) revolution in Russia, and it was feared that overcrowding and the continued existence of slums could lead to social unrest, if not revolution, in Britain. Thus the Housing Act of 1919, largely the work of Christopher Addison, President of the Local Government Board, placed a responsibility on local authorities to survey the housing needs within their area and build

'council' homes to fill the gaps. A housing manual was produced by the Local Government Board in 1920, laying down suggested standards of building and providing sample plans. It was

neither a corner shop at the end of the terrace, nor a public house nearby

written by Raymond Unwin, the architect responsible for Letchworth. However, Unwin now believed that the working class should be placed in low-density housing on the fringes of towns and cities, as the Walters Report had suggested.

Under the 1919 Act subsidies (grants) were given to the local authorities for each house built, but the scheme turned out to be costly and in the post-war slump Addison was dismissed and the grants reduced. These were nevertheless brought back in the Housing Acts of 1923 and 1924.

Thus in the inter-war years several large council estates were begun, the largest being at Becontree and at Downham, both on the fringes of London. In total, between 1919 and 1933–4 some three-quarters of a million council houses were built, which accounted for nearly one-third of all the houses built in Britain.

At Becontree in Essex, some 100,000 homes were built for families from east London by the LCC (London County Council), which collected rents and maintained the estate. The houses themselves were of a high standard, providing the families with the privacy and self-respect they had not had in the inner city. Now it was possible for the children to have a bedroom of their own, and no longer were there shared bathrooms and

outside toilets.

However, until the coming of the Ford Motor Works at Dagenham, the estate did not provide jobs and many had to travel by train to Charing Cross, a 75-minute journey before the District Line was extended, connecting Becontree with the Underground system. Not only was too much time spent travelling but many families missed the bustle of the city and urban life. The estate had very few facilities. There was neither a corner shop at the end of the terrace, nor a public house nearby. It was also some time before sufficient schools were built. Added to this, rents were high and many relations and friends had been left behind. Some 30,000 people left Becontree within the first ten years and 10,000 left in 1928–9 alone.

The Downham Estate was also established by the LCC and was on the southern boundaries of the borough of Lewisham, selected because its population was one of the lowest of all the metropolitan boroughs and it was well placed for the rail connection to London Bridge, Waterloo and Charing Cross from Grove Park. In 1918, the LCC formed a committee to look into the problem of housing after the war. They clearly had in mind the findings of the 1911 census, which had revealed that 50% of London's population was housed two to a room. Much of the worst housing was to be found south of the river in Bermondsey and Deptford, and the majority of Downham's population was rehoused from those areas. However, with the post-war depression, it was not until 1923 that the Grove Park Estate (Downham) was launched, largely through the provision of the 1919

Housing Act, whereby councils received housing subsidies.

Soon the necessary services were in place, such as a tramway through the middle of the estate to Grove Park station. In addition, schools, surgeries, churches, shops and parks were provided. All the houses were to be rented as follows:

2-room flat	9/-
3-room house	12/-
4-room house	12/6 to 14/-
5-room house	14/6 to 15/3

Building was very rapid:

	number of houses
1925	388
1926	1181
1927	2990
1928	4605
1929	5446
1930	6071

The average cost per house was £700, and the number of houses built by the LCC is indicated by the fact that on 19 February 1927, Queen Mary opened the 17,000th house constructed on the estate since the war.

Downham was built on rolling farmland, and with good transport connections. In addition the return fare to London was less than that from Becontree. None of the planners of the inter-war estates envisaged that the rehoused working class would eventually own motor cars. Thus, at Downham the main road through the estate was very wide to accommodate trams and buses, but many of the side roads and culs-de-sac were planned with wide pavements and fairly narrow roads to discourage through traffic. None of the houses had garages and today the occupants' cars are parked in the street or in gardens.

One of the interesting features of these two London estates, and of many others such as those on the outskirts of Manchester, Leeds and Sheffield, is that the houses themselves look very much the same, although there were a large number of different styles. In part the uniformity was brought about by the fact that the LCC did all the maintenance, from hedge cutting to house painting. No individual improvements were allowed.

The one shortcoming for many estate dwellers was that most of the amenities were on the fringes of the estate. Certainly there were far fewer convenient shops and public houses than in the densely populated inner-city areas.

In the 1980s the Conservative government encouraged the sale of council houses. How many of these houses on the Becontree Estate are now owned by their former tenants?

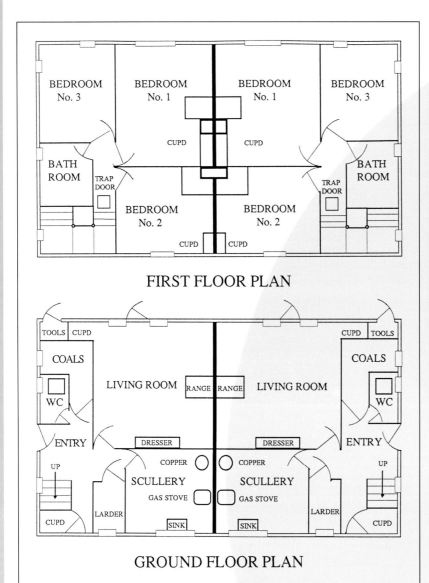

FIRST FLOOR PLAN

GROUND FLOOR PLAN

Plan of an inter-war council house. What advantages would the occupants of this house have had over a family living in a nineteenth-century slum?

Becontree Housing

Rooms	1	2	3	4 (without parlour)	4 (with parlour)	5	6	Total
Cottages	–	–	8,872	7,019	5,131	3,599	138	24,759
Cottage flats	8	749	208	42	31	21	–	1,059

Why do you think that the three- and four-roomed cottages were the most popular? How might the rooms have been used? Who would the cottage flats have been built for?

From Modern Housing Estates *by S. Gale (1949)*

The Downham Estate, Kent, under construction in the mid-1920s. Each house has a garden at the back and front. Although they all look the same, there are several differences. Can you spot them?

The Downham Tavern

December 1925: The Council resolved that a refreshment room and rooms for use for social events and meetings should be built. They propose to transfer a licence from the 'Osborne Arms' in the Watergate Street area of Deptford (already over supplied with licensed houses). This would be on a site at the junction of Bromley Road and Bromley Road by-pass.

November 1927: The above scheme was abandoned because the justices [the magistrates] refused to transfer the licence, and shops were built. Instead a new site was found, the area bounded by Downham Way, Moorside Road and Capstone Road, for a licensed refreshment house run by Barclay Perkins and Co. Ltd., while the Council will retain some control in order to enforce a suitable standard of conduct, thereby overcoming certain disadvantages inherent in older public houses.

The license for the Downham Tavern was granted on 1 May 1928. Why did the magistrates refuse to transfer the licence from Deptford?

Abridged from the LCC Housing Minutes

1 If your school is situated on an inter-war estate you could carry out a survey in your class to find out how many (a) students, (b) parents and (c) grandparents were born there. If they weren't, did they come from the inner city?

2 Estate housing often looks very uniform at first sight. Either sketch or take photographs of as many styles as you can find.

3 In the 1980s many council houses were sold to private owners. Try and identify these houses from external changes.

4 A number of local history groups have published interviews with those who remember council estates in the early days (e.g. the excellent *A Home of Our Own* by the Longley and Southey Group in Sheffield). You might like to compile a similar study, based on the memories of grandparents or neighbours, and containing early photographs and postcards.

MY LITTLE
METRO-LAND HOME

VOCAL ONE STEP.

WORDS BY.
BOYLE LAWRENCE.
MUSIC BY
HENRY THRAILE.

2/- NET

HERMAN·DAREWSKI·MUSIC·PUBLISHING·Co·
ST SWITHINS SYNDICATE LTD.
122–124 CHARING CROSS ROAD; LONDON .W.C.2.
AMERICA. LEO FEIST (INC) NEW YORK.

Sheet music cover, dating from before 1914. By this time building around the stations on the Metropolitan Line out of London was already under way, and the term 'Metroland' had been coined. How does the larger house seek to evoke the building styles of the past?

Journey time to work, the cost of travel and the length of one's working day determined whether one could move out. In the mid-nineteenth century, the expansion of the railway enabled people to live in growing suburbs such as Ealing and Wimbledon (in London), Edgbaston (Birmingham) and Dore (Sheffield) and travel daily into the city centre to work. However, it was the extension of the London Underground system and the electrification of many surface lines early this century that led to further expansion. The Metropolitan Railway carried out a vast advertising campaign in the decade before the First World War to publicize their services into rural Middlesex, Buckinghamshire and Hertfordshire. 'Metroland' promised the opportunity to live in a rural Arcadia and be able to travel easily and speedily to work each day.

We have seen how the large council estates began after 1919. Parallel to this expansion was the renewed development of the suburbs, where houses were built for sale or rent by a host of speculative builders in the inter-war years. Suburbs sprang up around the majority of our main towns and cities, stimulated by demand and by the quick profit they seemed to offer builders. Location was important, for many of the new residents were commuters who were seeking more space and a better environment on the fringes of the countryside. Hence areas such as south Lancashire and north

A suburb may be defined as a residential area on the outskirts of a town or city, from where the majority of people commute daily to work, usually in the town or city centre. They are therefore known as commuters. Suburbs are not peculiar to this century. In the early nineteenth century London was expanding outwards into areas such as Brixton and Camberwell, where new terraced houses were run up for the skilled working class, and semi-detached or detached villas for the professional groups. As industry and commerce grew, many city dwellers, not only in London, but also in such places as Glasgow, Manchester and Birmingham, moved outwards into more thinly populated areas or to estates where new houses were built.

Developments in transport clearly aided the expansion.

Cheshire were developed for commuters into Manchester and Liverpool, whilst the Chilterns and North Downs attracted many similar developments.

Middle-class families were much smaller in size than in Victorian times and they now sought homes that they could buy. Purchasers were aided in the 1930s by a decline in interest rates and an extended period of repayment, which could be as long as twenty-five years. What people wanted were mainly semi-detached or detached homes that were not identical to each other, houses that through different features and improvements were very clearly privately owned. Middle-class professional people and office workers moved into estates in which they bought homes on a mortgage according to their earnings. These were usually single family houses or bungalows, containing at least two bedrooms, and with a garden front and back. They were frequently built in traditional styles with mock-Tudor beams on the outside and coloured and leaded glass in the main windows.

One such estate was at Petts Wood, near Orpington in Kent, some fifteen miles from London. The development was due to one man, Basil Scruby, a self-taught developer, who had been looking for a suitable site on which to build a garden suburb. Petts Wood seemed ideal. It was a woodland area between Chislehurst and Orpington, but unfortunately, whilst the railway went through it, there was no station. After hard bargaining with the railway company, Scruby persuaded them to provide a halt (stopping place) at Petts Wood in February 1928. He himself had to supply the land for the future station and goods yard and also £6,000 towards the construction

of the station. Nevertheless Scruby was delighted, for the line had recently been electrified and the journey time was only thirty minutes into London Bridge, Waterloo or Charing Cross.

The initial station was very basic – uncovered and lit by oil lamps – and the platform was just long enough for an eight-carriage train. However, Scruby's judgement was correct and within sixteen years there were some 3,000 daily commuters into London. Petts Wood became a particularly popular place to live for those connected with the printing industry in Fleet Street,

the opportunity to live in a rural Arcadia

as it had some of the earliest and latest stopping trains, so they could get home in the early hours of the morning after the daily paper had been set.

Alongside the station, Scruby laid out a square around which shops were built in a half-timbered Tudor style. In the centre was his estate office, which became the hub of local development. Houses were restricted to a very low density per acre, and had to be built to a high specification. The black and white Tudor style was most popular, and the effect was to re-create the image of a romantic rural past in suburbia. In all some forty-five different builders were used, including Scruby's own Petts Wood Building Company. One such builder was Noel Rees, whose name today is still mentioned in the sales details of the houses he built. These were of a particularly high standard, with their Tudor features, leaded lights, beamed interiors and inglenooks. Interestingly, the railway line through Petts Wood came to be a social divide. On one side were the most expensive

larger houses, while on the other were pleasant but less costly smaller houses, mainly semi-detached, on smaller plots.

By 1939 many people had moved out of cities to live in their suburban dream. Their homes were fitted with the latest kitchen gadgets and there were power points for vacuum cleaners. They were truly family houses with machinery replacing the domestic servants of former times. However, there were problems. The motor car had brought ribbon development and it was not until 1935 that an act of Parliament sought to control it. In addition, many of the suburbs once separated from the urban areas came to suffer from in-filling, along and out from the main roads. Soon urban sprawl and the spread of the city into the countryside became an increasing problem as the train, bus and car enabled commuters to travel greater distances. To try to prevent this destruction of the countryside, the Green Belt was introduced, at first in the London area. It restricted development within a circle, or belt, around the city at a distance of approximately fifteen miles. It is still in being, but there is constant pressure upon it.

Sometimes different types of building led to conflict. As the Downham Estate (described on pp. 21–23) spread southwards, the residents of nearby Bromley built a wall to prevent any links between the council estate and themselves and to stop through-traffic. The wall illustrated the problems faced by the LCC in trying to house working-class people in what was becoming suburbia.

The Bromley Wall

It was about seven feet high and it had broken glass on the top. When I was a child I lived in the council houses and we used to climb over the wall because we used to scrump apples and throw things up at the conker trees to get the conkers down – there were trees over on the Bromley side, you see. And of course they didn't like us doing that, we got shouted at. As I grew older I realized how inconvenient the wall was for the mothers, because to catch a bus to Bromley they had to do a detour with the wall being there.

I used to live in the house next to the wall on the council side. One day a young girl decided it wasn't right to have a wall up there when there was a war imminent, and she decided she'd start knocking a lump off. I suppose there was a dozen teenagers around her, encouraging her, but the police came and stopped her.

The wall was taken down towards the latter part of the war because when we had air raids, ambulances couldn't get through.

The wall was built by homeowners across their road, which led into the Downham Estate. Why do you think they took such direct action?

Mrs Betty Trigg, quoted by G. Weightman and S. Humphries in The Making of Modern London 1914–1939 *(1984)*

These advertisements for rented accommodation in Metroland, to the north-west of London, were published around 1914. What claims are made by the advertisers for their properties? Why is distance from the station listed in each case?

UNDERGROUND

THE SOONEST REACHED AT ANY TIME
GOLDERS GREEN
(HENDON AND FINCHLEY)
A PLACE OF DELIGHTFUL PROSPECTS

Life in a north London suburb, as seen in a 1908 poster.

Southgate in Middlesex

There is probably no better situated residential district on the Northern heights of London than Southgate [with] its fine healthy position, about 400 feet above sea level, together with the splendid travelling facilities to and from the centre of London . . .

Although Southgate is practically on the very fringe of London, the air is there pure and bracing. There is no overcrowding of houses. The sanitation and water supply are both excellent . . . Many labour-saving features are incorporated in the design, whilst the solid and fireproof construction alone is unique in regard to private dwelling houses in England.

Occupying the finest and healthiest situation on the Arnos Park Estate, 7 minutes from the tube station, and about the same distance from the excellent shopping at The Green, Old Southgate.

List the advantages put forward of buying a house in Southgate. Which of them do you think would have had the most influence on a prospective buyer?

From London and Suburbs Old and New *by F. Green and S. Wolff, Souvenir Magazines (1934)*

Country Apartments.

NOTE.—The nearest Stations to the addresses given are shown in bold headlines.

NAME AND POSTAL ADDRESS.	To Let. Sitting rooms	To Let. Bed-rooms	Dist'nce from Station.	REMARKS.
HARROW-ON-THE-HILL.				
Miss Alexander, "Hillcrest," 70, Welldon Crescent.			3 mins.	"Shorthand, Typewriting, & Duplicating Bureau." Typewriting Machines lent on Hire.
Mr. & Mrs. Hunter, Lincoln House ..	5	10	1 mile	Splendid sit., every con., board optional, good cooking, well recommended.
EASTCOTE.				
Mrs. Rose Tobutt, South Hill Farm ..	2	2	1 mile	Very pretty country walks, near woods.
RUISLIP.				
Mrs. Mallett, The Stores, Ruislip Common.	1	2	1½ miles	Terms mod., bath, healthy spot, pretty country, apply full particulars.
Mrs. R. A. Rushfoutt, "Benvemi," Kingsend Avenue.	1	1	2 mins.	Bath, piano, good cooking and attendance
ICKENHAM.				
Mrs. Mothersole, Manor View Villas.	1	2	4 mins.	Terms mod., pretty country, board opt.
UXBRIDGE.				
"Gardner's Arms," Park Road, Uxbridge Common.	2	4	¼ mile	Teas with new laid eggs a speciality. Station Staff for directions.
PINNER.				
Miss Upham, Rose Bank, Love Lane.	2	2	5 mins.	Good cooking and attendance.
Mrs. Fred Jones, Raleigh, Waxwell Lane.	2	3	5 mins. walk.	Good position, suitable for Ladies or Gentlemen, board optional, bath.
NORTHWOOD.				
Mrs. Rowell, "Haytor," Chester Road.	1 or 2	3	5 mins.	Gocd position, bracing air, charming country, near woods and common.
Mrs. Longman, "Deercroft," Hallowell Road.	1	2	about 3 mins.	Near Church, Golf Links and Shops. Highly recommended.
Mrs. Soundy, "Roselea," Murray Road.	2	4	3 mins.	Bath (H. & C.), mod. san., electric light, board optional, excellent references.
Miss Howard, "Westville," Hollowell Road.	1	2 or 3	2 mins.	Bath (H. & C.), good cooking, board optional.
RICKMANSWORTH.				
Mrs. C. Collier, 76, Talbot Road. ..	1	1	8 mins.	Good cooking and attendance, board optional, Terms moderate, nr. park.
E. A. Turner, The Old Tannery House.	3	6	¾ mile	Lovely garden, weekend visitors, beautiful country walks, luncheons, motor accommodation.
Mrs. Talbert, The Red House, Drayton Ford.	1	3	1½ mile	Delightful sit. amidst orchards, woods, fishing and boating, lovely gardens.
Mrs. C. Sear, "Heatherdene," Croxley Green.	2	3	1 mile	Bath, nice garden, good cooking, board optional, good references.
Mrs. A. Cupper Mudd, "Ashwell," Yorke Road, Croxley Green.	2	2	1 mile	Bath (H. & C.), bracing, pretty district.
CHORLEY WOOD AND CHENIES.				
Mrs. Geoghegan, "Firdale," ..	1	2	7 mins.	Good cooking, quiet house, bath, nice garden, near golf links, moderate.
Miss C. King, "Inverness."	3	5	10 mins.	Detached on high ground, large garden, apartments or furnished house.
Mrs. Browton, "St. Margaret," Lower Road.	2	2	8 mins.	Close to common and church, board optional, terms moderate.
W. Westell, Red Lion Hotel, Chenies.	2	4	1½ mile	Pleasantly situated, good catering, highly recommended.
Miss Angus, "Clovelly," Haddon Road.	2	4	10 mins.	Bracing, charming country, high, pleasant situation, comfortable.
Mrs. A. Blareau, Laurel Cottage, Quickly Lane.	1	1	15 mins. walk.	Terms moderate, and pleasantly situated.
Mrs. Beavan, "Ardmore."	1	2	7 mins.	Terms moderate, conveniently situated, board optional, excellent references.
Mrs. E. Locke, "The Swallows." ..	2	2	10 mins.	Large garden, bath (H. & C.), up-to-date sanitation, good cooking.
Mrs. Wearing, Bulls Land Terrace, Heronsgate Road.	1	1 or 2	1 mile	Terms moderate.
CHESHAM.				
James Walker, Black Horse, Waterside.	1	3	1 mile	Overlooking River Chess, lawn, large orchard and garden.
Miss Lemon, "The Myrtle," Hawridge Common, Berkhamsted.	1	2	3½ miles	600ft. above sea level, splendid view, facing common, board optional.
E. E. Ford, 93, Turney Road, Dulwich, S.E.	1	3	1¾ miles	Furnished cottage, main water, common and golf links opposite.
Mrs. H. Batchelor, Fair View, Hivings Hill.	1	2	15 mins.	High and healthy position, bath (H. & C.) modern sanitation arrangements.
Mrs. A. Rickett, Shantock Farm, Bovingdon.	1	2	3½ miles	Ideal situation, piano, out-door sanitation, terms moderate.

Please mention METRO-LAND *when writing.*

52

1 Try to find someone who has lived in suburbia since the inter-war years. Ask them why their family moved there, where from, whether the house was new and what the area was like in the early days.

2 If you live in a suburb, write a few paragraphs for a leaflet such as that quoted in the sources, attracting people to the area.

3 What changes are likely to have been made to an inter-war house over the past fifty years? Think particularly about the kitchen, bathroom, heating, windows and carpets.

4 Do you think there are any disadvantages to life in suburbia, as compared with life in an inner-city area?

Detached inter-war homes in suburbia. Can you identify the traditional features in their exteriors?

By 1939 there were 12.7 million dwellings in Britain, 10% of them built by local authorities since 1919. Sadly, though, it would be wrong to assume that inter-war building in the private suburbs and on council estates had solved the housing crisis. There were still many people living in cramped and overcrowded conditions, and surveys suggested that much of the old housing was in need of demolition. Thus by 1939 a great deal remained to be done.

The Second World War (1939–45) put an end to both private and council building. Virtually every family had someone involved in either the armed forces or in civil defence. The civilian population was affected as it had not been in the First World War, and the mass bombing of our cities rendered many people homeless. Around 20,000 homes were destroyed and a further quarter of a million damaged. It was usually the densely crowded streets near the factories and the docks that suffered the most. Clearly, something had to be done when in 1945 and 1946 those who had served in the war returned to their families. Temporary accommodation in certain requisitioned buildings and pre-fabs was provided and some of the latter still remain today. But the people and the government wanted more. There was a general consensus (agreement) that Britain must not be allowed to return to the poverty, unemployment and inadequate housing of the 1930s.

The war itself had seen a growth in planning by the state: rationing, conscription, civil-defence regulations and identity cards were all introduced. What is more, they were seen to work in contributing to victory and it was in this mood that all political parties within the National Government embarked on a series of reforms. These, concerning education, the creation of the National Health Service and insurance legislation, laid the foundations for what we call the Welfare State. Much of the work was undertaken by the Labour government that came to power in 1945, but it was the Conservative wartime Prime Minister, Winston Churchill, who had said at the Mansion House on 9 November 1943: 'I regard it as a definite part of the duty and responsibility of this National Government to have it set about a vast and practical scheme to make sure that in the years immediately following the war, there will be food, work and homes for all.'

By 1945, the people expected action; planning was to be the key to what came to be called post-war reconstruction. Various wartime reports had shown what needed to be done, and the direction that should be taken. The first was by the Barlow Commission, which reported in January 1940. Its brief was to study the distribution of the industrial population. Pre-war unemployment was seen by many to be the result of *laissez-faire* by the government, which had made the Depression worse in the northern industrial areas. The Barlow Report called for national action and planning by a central authority; it dealt with the urban areas, where 80% of the population lived. The next report, by Lord Justice Scott in 1942, dealt with the land of England and Wales, of which 80% was still in agricultural use. It produced a virtual charter for the countryside and urged that planning should not wait upon the end of the war.

Following the heavy bombing of 1940, the Uthwatt Committee was established to look at the problem of compensation for war damage and the improvement of the environment in the subsequent rebuilding. When the Committee reported in 1942, its primary concern was seen to be national planning. It recommended that town-planning laws be amended to promote redevelopment by making it easier to acquire land. Redevelopment was to take place without high profits being made by speculators as the land values increased. The Committee also recommended that land values should be held at March 1939 levels.

In 1945 Sir William Beveridge opened an exhibition entitled 'Rebuilding Britain'. In his speech he argued that the opportunity for creating a new Britain had now arrived and that the old evils of poverty, unemployment and poor housing could be overcome by planning. However, twenty years before Beveridge's speech, efforts had already begun to regulate the growth of Britain's capital city. In November 1927, the Minister of Health, Neville Chamberlain, had established the Greater London Regional Planning Committee to look at the problems arising from decentralization and the spread of industry, together with the need for open spaces and a Green Belt around London. The Committee was also concerned with the question of ribbon development outward along the main roads, and two years later, in its first report, it stated:

> The capacity of main roads to carry modern traffic is dependent on the degree to which the stream of vehicles can be kept moving free from obstructions, as much as on the width of the roadway.

food, work and homes for all

Bomb damage in London in the Second World War. What type of buildings have been destroyed? What problems and opportunities resulted from destruction on this scale?

Hitherto when constructing arterial roads, adjacent owners have been left with unrestricted rights to use the frontage for building purposes, and to lay out as many branch roads as they desired.

Existing surburbs had expanded outwards from the local station, but now the motor car and bus had not only spawned garages, but created the potential for accidents and the ruin of the countryside. The report strongly recommended a Green Belt to surround London, together with regional planning to regulate development.

In April 1941, Lord Reith, the Minister of Works and Planning, asked the LCC to prepare a plan for London. The architects J.H. Forshaw and Professor Abercrombie were commissioned to do this, and the result was the County of London Plan (1943). Interestingly, and sadly, several of the problems exposed in the 1929 report still existed, and often in magnified form. Four major problems were identified: traffic congestion, depressed housing, inadequate and poorly distributed open spaces, and the unplanned way in which housing and industry had developed and intermingled. Many questions were raised in the report and many proposals made but the overriding message was that there must be planning, otherwise the lessons of the past would not be learnt. 'Haphazard planning is an extravagance: planning is sound business.'

In 1944 Professor Abercrombie put forward his Greater London Plan. This covered a much larger area than the County Plan. He now believed that three new factors had emerged from the war: the destruction of large areas, the evacuation of many people, and the industrial upheaval. The opportunity was there, thought Abercrombie, and the need for planning was critical. Homes must be provided, but they must be built in the right places. If they were too far from work, or were overcrowded, or grouped inadequately, or if they were without shopping centres and other facilities, they would spread indiscriminately over the countryside, causing more problems for the future. He agreed with Churchill that all citizens after the war should have homes, work and sufficient food. Nevertheless, care must be taken to avoid old mistakes. Estates surrounded by green fields, which were then built over within a few years, would only raise future problems.

Thus, by 1945, there was a mood of optimism and a general desire not to go back to the situation that had existed in the inter-war years. The bombing and destruction had provided the opportunity; what was needed was a carefully planned future.

The Barlow Report, 1940

National action is necessary.

A Central Authority, national in scope and character, is required.

The objectives of national action should be:

a) Continued and further redevelopment of congested urban areas.

b) Decentralization or dispersal both of industries and industrial population from these areas.

c) Encouragement of a reasonable balance of industrial development throughout Great Britain.

The continued drift of the industrial population of London and the Home Counties constitutes a social, economic and strategical problem which demands immediate attention . . . In cases where decentralization or dispersal is found desirable, how far should the following be encouraged or developed?

a) Garden cities or garden suburbs

b) Satellite towns

c) Trading estates

d) Further development of existing small towns or regional centres.

The time factor is important . . .

Do you think that the objectives of the report are still valid today? How far were the suggestions for promoting decentralization put into practice?

The Barlow Report, January 1940 (HMSO)

A Charter for the Countryside, 1942

A big rural housing programme should be undertaken.

Low cost electricity should be made available.

Special consideration should be given to the provision of a main water supply.

Steps should be taken to provide social centres in all villages.

Every village should be provided with playing fields.

National forest parks should be established.

Before new towns are established in country areas, vacant or derelict land in existing towns should be fully utilized.

Control should be exercised over the siting of advertisements.

All existing villages and country towns should be by-passed.

The Scott Report, August 1942 (HMSO)

Put the above list in order of importance. Justify your top three choices. Which of the recommendations have been implemented?

'The Homecoming', 1945. The soldier's family have been moved from their bomb-damaged home to a 'prefab'. Why were such dwellings given this nickname?

Rebuilding Britain

These, then, are the four stones which we must put in our sling before we set out to fight the giant Squalor: planned use of land, sane use of transport, right use of the architects and the maximum efficiency of the building industry . . . The drive for dealing with the giant Squalor must come from the people of the country . . . I hope that they'll come to feel that the conditions of crowding, discomfort, dirt, danger to health and daily exhaustion of travelling to and from work . . . are not worthy of Britain for the British . . . Now is the opportunity for making the New Britain that we all desire.

Address by Sir William Beveridge at the opening of the 'Rebuilding Britain' exhibition, quoted in Planning for Reconstruction, *c. 1945 (The Architectural Press)*

In the light of what you have read, support the arguments for the 'four stones' that Beveridge says are needed. Do you think the style of the speech well chosen for 1945?

▲ *Sir William Beveridge at a meeting in 1943. What sort of audience is he addressing and what might have been the subject of his speech?*

1 Find out what your area was like in 1945. Plot any widespread destruction by bombing. Try to identify rebuilding dating from the post-war years. (NB: Make sure you do not confuse this with recent inner-city redevelopment.)

2 See if you can find pre-war photographs of your area (postcards will be the most common) and compare them with the same scenes today. What has changed?

3 From your local reference library, try to obtain newspaper reports and, if possible, photographs of wartime bomb damage.

4 Design a poster in support of the aims of one of the reports mentioned in this chapter.

One of Abercrombie's suggestions in the Greater London Plan of 1944 was to create four rings around London, which would determine future development. Surrounding the county of London would be an inner urban ring and then a suburban ring, both of which were already developed. These would be circled by a substantial Green Belt, which would include various established towns. Beyond this would be an outer country ring. Abercrombie's main objective was similarly adopted by planners looking at the other major cities and towns: namely that the inner cities should not expand any further in terms of either population or industry. This would ensure lower-density housing in more congenial surroundings and, it was hoped, reduce the numbers commuting into the cities. Equally, by pursuing a policy of decentralization, the government could locate new employment in certain named areas, thus avoiding the problem of further urban sprawl.

Abercrombie suggested that the new (satellite) towns should be built at a distance of approximately thirty miles around London. They were to contain a maximum of 60,000 people. This recommendation was not acted upon by the wartime National Government but, after the 1945 Labour victory, the New Towns Act was passed in November 1946. Stevenage in Hertfordshire was named as the first New Town, and in the next four years thirteen more were chosen. Over

The interior of the shopping centre in Milton Keynes, a New Town in north Buckinghamshire, founded in 1967. Why do many people prefer to shop in surroundings like these? What effect might this have on other shops in the area?

half were in the London area, with two others being in Scotland, two in the North East, one in Wales, and one in the Midlands. However, they were not to be entirely based on the principles laid down by Ebenezer Howard. New Town corporations were formed and, in the spirit of the first post-war Labour government, private initiative played a minor role. In part this was thought to be necessary in order to override local objections and speed the planning process. The development corporation for each town was to be formed and financed by central government. The corporation was given powers of compulsory purchase and was to link with the existing local authority to build houses. The sum of £50 million was set aside to initiate the programme. Each named town was surrounded by its Green Belt, which Howard would have welcomed.

The Labour government sought to learn from experience and proposed to avoid urban sprawl outwards from our cities. The Town Planning Act of 1947 was intended to prevent large-scale unplanned development. It empowered counties and county boroughs to carry out surveys and draw up plans. Planning was to be concerned not only with existing industrial sites and residential areas, but also with the green fields and farmland. The countryside could now be preserved as such, whilst in areas of development, local authorities could identify portions for open space and leisure. The Green Belt had been protected by legislation, and in 1949 the National Parks and Access to the Countryside Act sought to preserve and improve designated rural areas.

The New Towns were designed to provide new opportunities and a new life for urban dwellers. In the 1950s a second phase began and in 1963 two of the most famous towns were founded: Dawley (now Telford) in Shropshire, and Milton Keynes in Buckinghamshire. In each, shopping precincts, health centres and schools were planned and the residential and industrial areas were strictly divided.

Some New Towns, such as Cumbernauld in Dunbartonshire, were built on green-field sites. Others, such as Telford, were largely developed by in-filling existing villages. A further difference centred on the expansion of industrial villages and towns, such as Madeley and Wellington, both close to Telford, which also attracted overspill population from Birmingham. Cumbernauld was built to house people from the slums of Glasgow, especially the Gorbals. It was established in 1956 and built on a hill in open country. The huge town centre contained all amenities from supermarkets to council offices. One feature later adopted by other developments was the separation of traffic and pedestrians, creating pedestrian-free areas, pedestrian walkways and underpasses. Not only were road accidents thus avoided, but the danger from exhaust emissions was also reduced. However, there remained a major problem in Cumbernauld: its failure to attract sufficient industry to support its population. Many people found themselves having to travel back into Glasgow to work.

new opportunities and a new life for urban dwellers

Lack of employment was not the only drawback to life in New Towns. Abercrombie and other planners had not anticipated the post-war baby boom. In fact, they had expected the population to remain steady, but the reverse happened with the result that they failed to provide sufficient houses: only 175,000 were built in the New Towns between 1946 and 1970. Another problem faced by New Towns was their age structure. Older people were reluctant to move and thus the towns were populated by young married couples, many of whom had moved in order to bring up their children in a more pleasant environment. This led to pressure on schools to provide more places, and, in some cases in the 1990s, has resulted in an ageing population.

Comments on New Towns

Compared with the rest of the country as a whole [New Towns are] socially unbalanced in quite the opposite direction from that which is generally assumed. They have a preponderance of lower-middle and middle income families. It would be a valid criticism that they have given too little – almost negligible – help with the housing of the poorer families of unskilled workers in London, and perhaps in Glasgow.

From an article by Wyndham Thomas in The Regional City *(1966)*

It's a good place to live if you can afford it. I wouldn't like to go back to Glasgow, but because of high prices this place is becoming less of a lung for the slums of Glasgow and more of a middle-class area.

Cumbernauld resident, reported in the Daily Worker, *29 March 1966*

What criticisms of the New Towns do these two extracts have in common? The *Daily Worker* was a Communist paper. Does this make the comment of little value or not?

A View of Crawley

Crawley in West Sussex was designated a New Town in 1947. At the time it had 10,000 inhabitants, along with the villages of Ifield and Three Bridges. By 1963 the town had grown to 60,000. The architectural historian Nikolaus Pevsner described it as follows:

> It was a good idea to make the existing High Street the spine of the new development, place the town centre immediately to its side and make it essentially pedestrian. Yet for the visual well-being of the High Street, things have not worked out so well . . .
> However well conceived the idea of an old High Street in juxtaposition with [next to] the new

shopping centre was, in the end the High Street was badly mauled by it, i.e. by traffic and parking mainly. One can just recognize how nice the street must once have been . . .

Pevsner went on to describe the housing in Crawley:

> Bricks of divers [varied] colours are used, brown, reddish, yellow, and also whitewash . . . old trees are carefully preserved, sometimes whole rows of them. Yet uniformity cannot be avoided, even if it is a friendly, cosy, reassuring uniformity with nothing regimented about it . . . What is needed is every time almost identical: a row of shops, a pub., a church or chapel.

From The Buildings of England: Sussex *by Ian Nairn and Nikolaus Pevsner (1965)*

The view expressed is a personal one written thirty years ago. Why, then, are the comments still useful?

New housing at Aycliffe, Co. Durham in 1955. The houses on this estate were built 14 to the acre, a high density for the town. What sort of residents might they attract? What might be under construction in the top right-hand corner of the photograph?

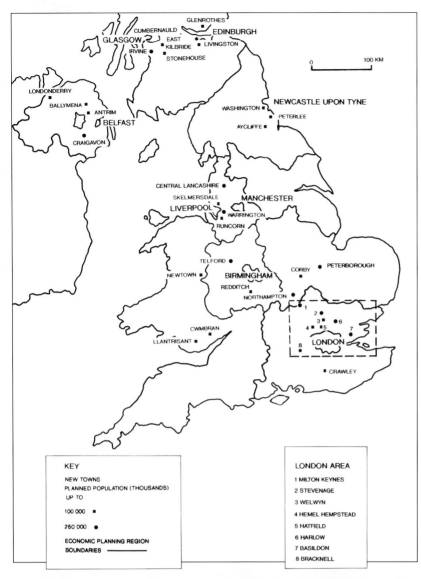

KEY

NEW TOWNS
PLANNED POPULATION (THOUSANDS)
UP TO

100 000 ■

250 000 ●

ECONOMIC PLANNING REGION
BOUNDARIES ——————

LONDON AREA

1 MILTON KEYNES
2 STEVENAGE
3 WELWYN
4 HEMEL HEMPSTEAD
5 HATFIELD
6 HARLOW
7 BASILDON
8 BRACKNELL

New Towns in Britain. The majority were created following the New Towns Act of 1946. Others, such as Northampton and Warrington, were old towns that had undergone redevelopment, while Welwyn, which had been planned as a garden city, was redesignated a New Town.

1 Visit one of the New Towns shown on the map. Take a camera and make a photographic record of buildings. When you return note down your general impressions. The information centre or reference library should be able to provide you with an overall plan or map on which you can note the buildings you photographed.

2 What advantages and disadvantages have been experienced by those living in New Towns? Draw up two lists to compare these.

3 Study the map of New Towns and compare it with the map of Britain in your atlas. Can you say why New Towns were built in particular areas?

4 Many New Towns no longer fulfil their original purpose. Corby in Northamptonshire housed many steel workers when that industry was flourishing. In the 1980s the town had to attract new industries and activities. Try and find out how this was achieved. What other New Towns have had to change direction?

In spite of the work of the New Town corporations and of attempts to prevent urban sprawl, by 1950 seven conurbations could be identified: Birmingham, Tyneside, Clydeside, the West Riding, Manchester, Merseyside and London. This term means simply an area of continuous urban development, including and connecting two or more towns. It was first used by Professor Patrick Geddes, who had argued that an area should be studied by reference to its past. Only when this was done was it possible to project into the future. Thus the report *Conurbations: A Planning Survey of Birmingham and the Black Country*, published in 1948 and drawing on Geddes's ideas, began with an account of the way in which the area had been affected by the Industrial Revolution. This had clearly brought prosperity to Birmingham and the Black Country but at considerable cost to the environment and the landscape. By 1948 the conurbation covered 270 square miles and had a population of 2 million people. Industry was so deeply rooted, and the people so dependent on it, that there was no question of it being relocated. Equally, the existing cities, towns and villages were there to stay. Realistically, the planners sought to improve the old and at the same time develop the new. Over the years some industries had grown, while others had fallen into decline. Thus the *Conurbations* survey found that there was a large acreage of derelict land – spoil heaps, ponds, abandoned factories, defunct canals and polluted rivers – which could be transformed to answer the needs both of housing and leisure, so protecting the remaining open space. Geddes argued that rather than allowing indiscriminate

sprawl outwards from the city centre into the countryside, planners should seek to push the country into the town wherever possible.

Ideas such as these were also put into practice in London. The

people are unwilling to venture out alone

first review of the County of London Plan of 1943 was published in 1960. In it were listed forty-seven new open spaces which the LCC had acquired since 1951, one of them being the grounds of Holland House in Kensington; an area of over fifty acres, it became a public park rather than being sold for housing. Where redevelopment after the bombing had taken place, smaller 'lungs' were

created. Part of the Roman wall that had surrounded the City of London was now exposed to the north of the Tower. In order to display it, a small paved park with seats was created. Similarly, at Greenwich, the land surrounding the clipper ship the *Cutty Sark* was paved so that the ship could be seen to the best advantage.

By the 1950s Londoners were being rehoused in new dwellings at the rate of 50,000 a year. Many of these were in private housing projects, but the majority were in council houses and flats. Nevertheless, by 1956, 126,000 families still needed housing, due to slum clearance, road improvements and school building. The most popular solution was for planned estates in which there would be a combination of low-level housing

and what we now call high-rise or tower blocks. One of the main proponents of the latter was the influential French architect Le Corbusier. Planners noted that in the older urban areas many of the houses were no more than two storeys in height. Thus in the poorer districts many people were crammed together in narrow, ill-lit streets. The street was the only play space for children, which could have dangerous consequences. If the terraced rows were turned on end, the same number of dwellings could be produced, leaving space to surround them with open ground. In other words high-rise flats would retain the same densities per acre but would provide play areas and a much better environment.

Many such developments were built in the 1960s and 1970s, not only in London, but in virtually all our towns and cities. Some received international recognition. Park Hill (1961) was built on land overlooking the centre of Sheffield, and won awards, yet by the 1990s it had become unpopular with many of its inhabitants.

Similar high-rise developments are now often felt to be unsafe, particularly at night, with their concrete walkways and dark areas. The lifts are subject to abuse or lack of maintenance, people are unwilling to venture out alone, whilst families with children fear the long walk down to the play areas. Many older people contrast the high-rise flats with the homely terraced streets from which they came, with the pub and the corner shop and neighbours chatting in the street. Whether this is an idealized vision

of the past is irrelevant, as such views influence people's feelings about the present.

Another factor leading to change was the gas explosion in a tower block called Ronan Point in the East End of London in 1968, which caused several deaths. In addition, the rise in the price of fuel, especially electricity, in the 1970s led many people to abandon the systems that had been installed, such as under-floor heating, and use cheaper alternatives. This resulted in condensation problems.

In 1955 Duncan Sandys, the Conservative Minister of Housing, launched a major slum-clearance programme which was to continue for the next twenty years. Many towns and cities were keen to keep their population in order to reverse the trend towards suburbia. They were now required by government legislation to designate Green Belts to contain urban growth. To this end, governments from the mid-1950s onwards provided subsidies (cash aid) which gave builders three times as much for a flat in a fifteen-storey block as for a house. Many building firms, using prefabricated units, tendered for these lucrative contracts and the result can be seen today in the large number of high-rise council flats. The popular press and other commentators are certain of the reason why their building continued for so long: the architects were middle-class people who did not understand working men and women and did not themselves have to live in high-rise council flats. The historian sees the answer as being more complex.

Part of the vast Park Hill Estate in Sheffield, built between 1953 and 1961. The planners hoped the greens surrounding the high-rise blocks would be used by children.

Birmingham – 200 Years Ago

200 years ago, various industries sprouted simultaneously in the Midlands. The sword and gun makers of Birmingham, the smiths of Dudley, and the lorimers of Walsall, staked their claim without any thought of planning. Trades rose and flourished. Local coal pits supplied forge and furnace. The mine, the slag-heap and the quarry marred the surface of a pleasant countryside. Factories spread in ribbon development along the canal bank and the railway track. The iron works displaced the plough . . . until by the middle of the 19th Century 1000's of acres had been consumed.

From Conurbations: A Planning Survey of Birmingham and the Black Country, *West Midland Planning Group (1948)*

G. May was a German visitor to Britain. Here is an extract from his diary for 1814:

The whole district between Wolverhampton and Birmingham is covered with coal pits and ironworks, steam engines are to be seen all over the place. The fields are covered with soot and the air is polluted with smoke so that little can grow. It is hard to find a green leaf on the trees and hedges. Some parts of the district look as if they were suffering from a destructive fire.

Quoted by W.O. Henderson in Industrial Britain under the Regency *(1968)*

In what ways does the second extract support the statements made in the first? Do you think the Industrial Revolution would have spread so quickly if there had been town planning?

Ronan Point in Canning Town, east London, was severely damaged by a gas explosion in May 1968. What would residents of other high-rise flats have felt about this tragedy?

Croydon, south London, was extensively redeveloped in the late 1960s, as this photograph from a high-rise office block shows. Thirty years on, Croydon is now considering schemes for making the functional concrete blocks more attractive.

◀

Advantages of High Buildings

High buildings can have the advantages of open layouts with green open spaces and the maximum public use of the ground; good lighting; good vision from the upper storeys; freedom from noise; good air; and architectural interest. In residential areas, high blocks of flats give a high density for a small site and make possible a mixed development for the whole area, with a greater proportion of lower dwellings with gardens.

Write a similar paragraph on the disadvantages of high buildings. What measures could be taken to improve life for those in high-rise buildings?

From County of London Development Plan *(first review, 1960)*

1 If you live in a conurbation, see whether there was an early planning survey of your area. If so, compare it with the same area today.

2 Try and discuss, with relatives or friends, what it is like to live in a high-rise block, and/or look for articles and comments in the local or national papers.

3 Grants are now being made to improve the outward appearance of high-rise blocks. Sometimes this has been achieved by external decoration. See if you can find examples of such improvements in your area, and decide whether you consider the changes important.

4 If you were an architect given the task of designing a new development, what would you retain from the past, which 'mistakes' would you rectify, and what new ideas would you incorporate?

In the 1980s, under the Conservative government of Margaret Thatcher, home ownership was actively encouraged, and people did not need much persuasion to buy. A house or flat seemed to be an asset that would automatically increase in value over the years. As a result of legislation passed in the mid-1980s, local authorities were required to sell council houses and flats to their tenants. The price was determined by the length of the period during which rent had been paid, and big discounts were available to those who had lived in their homes for many years. Another incentive took the form of tax advantages given to couples who jointly purchased a house. The 1980s were boom years in which land and property values soared.

Property developers and local builders now began to scour the sought-after areas for building land, frequently making offers that owners found difficult to refuse. Houses with large gardens were purchased for demolition, and plots were bought on the outskirts of towns and villages. The latter practice often led to protests by individuals or pressure groups against the granting of planning permission. Increased car ownership meant that people were less dependent on public transport, and homeowners began to move away from overcrowded, expensive parts of the country, such as London and the Home Counties, to more distant rural areas. Frequently they would retain the same job and drive to the nearest station in order to commute to work each day. The effect of such changes was twofold. Those living in communities where new housing was being proposed were often

against further expansion, and the acronym NIMBY (Not In My Back Yard) came into fashion to describe those who were acting in their own interests. On the other hand, the rise in house prices in previously low-cost areas left many local residents (and especially young people) unable to afford to buy a home in their own towns and villages.

As we have seen in earlier

The 1980s were boom years . . . land and property values soared

chapters, much of the housing built during the inter-war and immediate post-war periods took the form of semi-detached properties and ribbon development, with long rows of houses having front and back gardens separated from those of their neighbours. However, the last two decades have seen a significant change. Approximately 40% of new private housing is detached and only 20% semi-detached. Demand among the affluent is very much for the individual property, often in culs-de-sac with names such as Dene, Close or Copse, giving a rural flavour. In such developments, houses are frequently built in a mock-Tudor or neo-Georgian style, with open-plan gardens at the front and without fences to divide the properties. Each house may be subtly different and, though there may be little space between them, the superior status of the detached house is reflected in its price.

At a national level, groups such as the Council for the Protection of Rural England have expressed concern at the continued encroachment into the countryside. However, although the number of people living in the

countryside is increasing, the number of traditional farming jobs is falling each year. Since the late 1980s the government has sought to boost employment in rural areas by lifting planning restrictions on sites in order to permit change of use. The results of this policy have been seen in, for example, the building of golf courses and the conversion of derelict barns for housing.

Powerful arguments are put forward regarding the building of new houses. Some would say that all those who want to live in the country should be allowed to do so. Others emphasize that if the vacant plots and derelict factories in the city centres were developed, the countryside could be preserved and traffic problems would decrease due to the decline in long-distance commuting.

The early 1990s have seen a slump in the housing market. Many people who bought when prices were high now have a mortgage higher than the present value of their house. Rising unemployment has added to the problem, as those who are not able to keep up their mortgage repayments may have their homes repossessed by the bank or building society that lent them the money. The rapid rise in interest rates up to 1992 also proved too much for many homeowners, especially if linked with the loss of a job or a reduction in overtime.

During the boom years of the 1980s, private property was also expensive to rent. The demand for affordable rented accommodation increased, particularly as the government did not allow money raised from the sales of council houses to be used to build new homes for rent.

London's Liverpool Street Station was built in the nineteenth century as a terminus for lines from eastern England, and is much used by commuters from Essex and beyond. It has recently been modernized. Do you think the blend of old and new is effective?

Thus by the late 1980s, many towns and cities had homeless people. Some had come in search of work, which they could not find, while others earned insufficient in unskilled part-time work to afford accommodation. Local authorities in urban areas have been forced to rent rooms for families in bed and breakfast hotels until more permanent homes can be found. At the very bottom of the scale are those who live on the streets or sleep in hostels provided by local authorities or religious groups.

In recent years there have been severe riots and disturbances in the inner-cities and on various council estates in towns as diverse as Oxford, Newcastle and Manchester. Many of these areas have large numbers of unemployed young people and the relationship between crime, unemployment and poverty is hotly debated.

Whilst the government has been reluctant to support local-authority housing, it has backed other initiatives such as housing associations, 2,300 of which now provide more than 600,000 homes for people in need. The aim is to provide good, low-rent accommodation, sometimes in newly built houses and flats, or alternatively in older houses that have been renovated. Another development has been the creation of Housing Action Trusts (HATs) under the provisions of the 1988 Housing Act. The idea is for the Trusts to take over control of run-down local-authority housing. The properties are then managed by private boards, which seek to improve them and make them attractive to tenants. In the summer of 1992, residents of over 5,000 homes in Liverpool voted to become the largest HAT to date. Significantly, they live in sixty-seven tower blocks. Likewise, tenants in Waltham Forest, east London, have also formed a HAT, which intends to use the government grant to demolish four estates of multi-storey blocks and replace them by houses with gardens.

Another initiative, tackling redevelopment on a larger scale, was the creation in the 1980s of Enterprise Boards, introduced in an effort to bring private investment into run-down areas. Private corporations were to take over planning from the local council and apply market forces to speed up development. The first such body was the London Docklands Corporation, founded in 1981, which developed derelict riverside areas in east London during the boom years of the 1980s. In addition, the 1990s have seen the introduction of the City Challenge, in which local authorities have been encouraged to submit plans for the regeneration of their area. Lewisham in south London was one of the first winners of a grant under this scheme. Critics argue that whilst such initiatives are to be welcomed, much more needs to be done to regenerate our inner cities and to provide homes for low-income families.

Executive Housing

In May 1993 a property developer placed the following advertisement in local newspapers in the London area:

—— is dedicated to creating the best possible living environments.

The flair and skill of ——'s planning, architectural and landscaping teams, give every development, and each new home, a unique and mature appeal.

A palette of traditional building materials and hand crafted finishes combine with inspired interior layouts that are fresh and alive with interest.

Meticulous attention to detail in interior finishes and features ensures that every —— home is full of character and charm whilst being extremely economical to heat and maintain.

——'s new homes are subject to very rigorous standards of workmanship and every new home has a full NHBC 10 year Warranty.

Come and see the Master Housebuilder for yourself.

Which groups is the advertisement appealing to? List the features that would generate interest among potential buyers.

"Research showed that amongst babies born to women living in bed and breakfast accommodation there were more premature births, more infant breathing problems, lower than average birth weights and more feeding problems."

THE FIGURES THAT DON'T MAKE SENSE*	
The annual cost of bed and breakfast accommodation for a homeless family.	£17,000
The cost of bringing an empty property back into use.	£13,000
The number of privately owned homes lying empty.	586,800
The number of local authority homes lying empty.	112,000
The number of people registered as homeless.	450,000

Shelter
THE NATIONAL CAMPAIGN FOR HOMELESS PEOPLE

◄ *The Castlefield area of Manchester is an example of successful urban redevelopment. In the foreground is the canal basin, and behind this the original booking office of the Liverpool and Manchester Railway, opened in 1830.*

▲ *What conclusion does this advertisement, which appeared in national newspapers in May 1993, wish you to draw from the figures? What arguments might the government use to defend its housing policy?*

Housing Action Trusts in North Hull

Mrs Nora Short in north Hull was the first tenant to have her flat improved. Residents were given a certain number of points to spend, and inspected show houses in order to see the various improvements on offer.

Inside the flat where she has lived for the past 15 years, the bathroom has a new suite and is fully tiled. The kitchen has new units, the walls are papered and the floors have new carpets. There is also a new gas fire, wall-mounted lights, gas central-heating and added insulation, and double-glazed windows. A new intercom links to a warden charged with looking after elderly residents.

'I can't describe the difference,' Mrs Short says. 'It's much warmer than it used to be. It used to be terribly cold in the bedroom and the bathroom used to be damp.'

Why might residents prefer to choose improvements themselves? Do you think that improvement is better than demolition?

From an article by Rachel Kelly published in The Times, *19 August 1992*

A detached house of the 1990s. Note how the built-in garage has reduced the remaining ground area.

1 Find out whether any schemes have taken place or are proposed in your area to develop land no longer serving its original purpose. These might include the conversion of old warehouses, docks or factories.

2 Your local newspaper or free paper will contain details of new housing, and estate agents will also provide information. Make up a file of advertisements over the course of a month. Which are private developments and which have been built for a council or housing association? You may also find the local reference library useful.

3 Many national charities are involved in providing housing and temporary accommodation for the poor. These include Shelter, Oxfam, the Salvation Army and Christian Aid. Find out whether any of these are working in your area – you can obtain their addresses from a telephone directory or reference library.

4 If you live in the country, or near it, study a modern Ordnance Survey map of your area and compare it with an older (preferably pre-war) map. Try and identify the main changes that have taken place.

1801 The first census carried out

1831 First cholera outbreak in Britain; 31,000 die

1835 The Municipal Corporations Act; town councils elected for the first time

1842 Chadwick's *Inquiry into the Sanitary Conditions of the Labouring Population* published

1845 Health of Towns Report published

1848 Public Health Act enables local Boards of Health to be formed

1861 Sheffield abolishes building of new back-to-back houses

1862 Peabody Trust formed, providing flats in urban areas

1863 Completion of Saltaire, the model village founded by Titus Salt

1867 Artisans', Labourers' and General Dwellings Company formed

1875 Artisans' Dwellings Act enables local authorities to draw up improvement schemes for slum clearance

1884 Octavia Hill at work in Southwark

1886 Charles Booth begins survey of the London poor

1888 Port Sunlight begun by Lord Leverhulme
London County Council formed

1890 Public Health Act passed – first act covering the construction of houses and local-authority building; Boundary Estate, Bethnal Green, founded (under 1890 Act)

1893 Bournville begun by George Cadbury

1898 Ebenezer Howard's *Tomorrow* published, proposing garden cities and towns

The Weavers' Triangle, Burnley, Lancashire. The earlier photograph was taken around 1900. What is the most striking difference between the two pictures? What does this tell you about the ways in which life has changed in the town during the twentieth century?

1899–1902 Second Boer War; 25% of volunteers judged unfit for service

1899 Garden City Association formed

1901 Seebohm Rowntree's *Poverty: A Study of Town Life* published

1902 Letchworth Garden City begun in Hertfordshire

1906–16 Liberals in power; they embark on a programme of social reform

1906 Hampstead Garden Suburb begun

1909 Housing and Town Planning Act passed

1914–18 First World War

1919 Addison's Housing Act provides government help for the building of council houses

1921 LCC housing estate begun at Becontree in Essex

1924 LCC housing estate begun at Downham in Kent

1926 Welwyn Garden City begun

1938 Green Belt Act passed to preserve the countryside from developers

1939–45 Second World War

1940 Barlow Report on industrial areas

1942 Scott Report on agricultural land in England
Uthwatt Report recommends town-planning laws to promote redevelopment of bomb-damaged areas

1946 New Towns Act passed

1947 Town Planning Act passed to stop ribbon development

1948 Nationalization of railways; British Rail replaces private companies

1949 National Parks and Access to the Countryside Act passed

1959 Britain's first motorway, the M1, opened between London and Birmingham

1968 Ronan Point tower block explosion

1977 Green paper on housing estimates that 200,000 units of housing per year will be needed during the 1980s

1979 Conservative government returned under Mrs Thatcher

1980 Housing Act gives tenants the right to buy their council houses; Enterprise Zones created

1981 London Docklands Corporation formed

1988 Housing Action Trusts (HATS) created. Local-authority tenants can now transfer the control of their homes from the council to housing associations or private landlords

1991 Ronan Point and seven neighbouring tower blocks dismantled

1992 North Hull HAT hands over first improved home to tenant

1993 Admiral's Reach opened. This is a joint venture between Newham Council, east London, and private developers, under which 320 new houses and apartments have been built on the site of Ronan Point and its neighbouring blocks
One million homes estimated to be unfit for occupation
Around 8,000 people sleeping rough in Britain
Over 60,000 people living in temporary housing

arable   land used for crops as opposed to pasture
Arcadia   a term derived from Greek and Roman poetry, meaning an idyllic rural setting
artisan   a skilled worker

back-to-back houses   terraces built with a common back wall and thus having no through ventilation
bye-laws   rules made by local authorities relating to matters such as the width of new roads, density of housing, fire regulations, etc.

census   the count of people taken each decade since 1801 (except for 1941)
cholera   a highly infectious and dangerous disease

decentralization   the process by which central government passes some of its powers to lesser bodies
dividend   the profit made on one's shares

ground rent   rent paid to landlords for use of their land

HMSO   His (Her) Majesty's Stationery Office, responsible for printing government publications

Industrial Revolution   the period between approximately 1780 and 1850, during which Britain became an industrial nation

in-filling   building on empty spaces, such as waste ground or gardens, in an area that has already been developed
inglenook   a recessed corner by the chimney

LCC   the London County Council, formed in 1888
laissez-faire   non-interference in a particular problem or issue
laths   wooden strips that, along with the plaster or hardened cow dung, formed the walls of houses before the Industrial Revolution
lorimer   a maker of the metal parts of a horse harness

migrant   a person who moves to another area
mortgage   the money lent to purchase a house and repaid with interest over a number of years

NHBC   the National House Building Council

prefabs   prefabricated buildings, i.e. buildings whose sections are built in a factory and assembled on site

radicalism   an extreme opinion, especially in politics
ribbon development   single-depth building along main routes out of built-up areas

scullery   in older houses, a room where kitchen jobs were done
squalor   the condition of being filthy, foul or neglected
slums   the worst areas of poor housing (sometimes called the Rookeries)
smith   a worker in metal
speculative builder   a builder who builds for profit, hoping that he will be able to sell or rent the properties
Swing Riots   riots against the threshing machine and low wages, which began in Kent and spread through the Home Counties in 1830. Named after the fictitious Captain Swing, 'author' of anonymous threatening letters sent to farmers who used the new machinery

tied cottage   a cottage belonging to the landowner, which was rented out to the labourer whilst in his employment
threshing machine   a machine that enabled corn to be threshed, thus saving labour and wages

Further Reading

There are very few specific books on this subject at the school level, though many general text books have a chapter. These are the books I have found particularly useful:

S. Anginotti (ed.), *A Home of Our Own: Langley and Southey Estates*, Sheffield Adult Education (*c.* 1990)

C. Booth, *Life and Labour of the London Poor* (final volume), Macmillan (1902)

A. Burton, *Cityscapes*, André Deutsch (1990)

E. Chadwick, *Sanitary Conditions of the Labouring Population*, HMSO (1842)

N. Fairbrother, *New Lives, New Landscapes*, The Architectural Press (1970)

P. Green and S. Wolff, *London and Suburbs*, Souvenir Press (1935)

P. Hall, *Cities of Tomorrow*, Blackwell (1988)

J. Lowe, *Welsh Country Workers*, National Museum of Wales (1988)

– *Welsh Industrial Workers' Housing 1755–1875*, National Museum of Wales (1989)

J. Madge, *People in Towns*, BBC Books (1968)

N. Morgan, *Vanished Dwellings: Preston*, Mullion Books (1990)

A. Quiney, *House and Home*, BBC Books (1986)

J. Reynolds, *Saltaire* (City Trail no. 2) Bradford Art Galleries and Museums (1980)

B.S. Rowntree, *Poverty: A Study of Town Life*, Macmillan (1901)

D. Stenhouse, *Understanding Towns*, Wayland (1977)

J.N. Tarn, *Working-Class Housing in Nineteenth-Century Britain*, Lund Humphries (1971)

R. Tubbs, *The Englishman Builds*, Penguin (1945)

P.J. Waller, *Town, City and Nation: England 1850–1914*, Oxford University Press (1983)

Acknowledgements

The Author and Publishers would like to thank the following for their kind permission to reproduce illustrations: Mary Evans Picture Library, pp. 5, 8, 14–15; Mullion Books, p. 7; Mansell Collection, pp. 10, 12; the Architectural Association, pp. 16, 17, 18, 19, 36–7; David Pratt, pp. 20–1, 32, 41; the Museum of London, p. 24; the London Transport Executive, p. 26; Hulton Deutsch Collection Ltd, pp. 29, 30–1, 38; Shelter, p. 42; Bryant Homes, p. 43; Brian Hall, p. 44; also Jim Pipe and Dave Davis (illustrators) for the house plan on p. 22 and the map on p. 35 respectively.

The cover painting is *St Pancras Hotel and Station from Pentonville Road* by John O'Connor, reproduced by permission of the Bridgeman Art Library. The cover photograph is by Sam Lambert.

Thanks go to the *Changing Britain* series editors for advice and editorial input: Alan Evans and Michael Rawcliffe.

Page numbers in **bold type** refer to illustrations